ABC's of Kindergarten
Alphabet Trace & Color Book
ISBN: 979-8-9896978-2-3

Martin's Children's Books LLC
www.martinchildrensbooks.com

All rights reserved.
This book or parts thereof
may not be reproduced in any form,
stored in a retrieval system, or
transmitted in any form by any means -
electronic, mechanical, photocopy,
recording, or otherwise-without prior
written permission of the publisher,
except as provided by the United
States of America copyright law.

ABC's

of Kindergarten Alphabet

TRACE and COLOR

Workbook

THIS BOOK BELONGS TO

_____

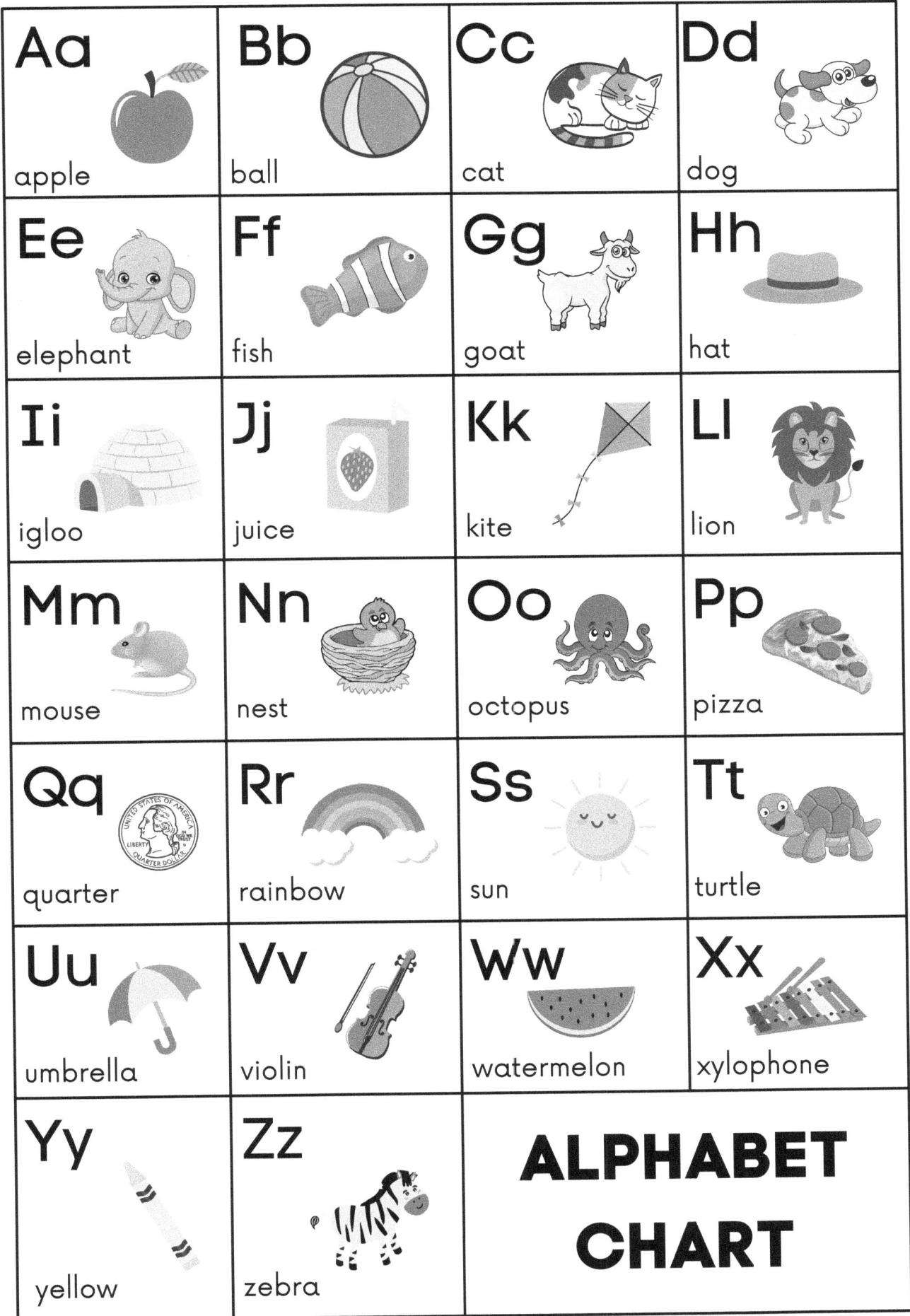

Aa apple	Bb ball	Cc cat	Dd dog
Ee elephant	Ff fish	Gg goat	Hh hat
Ii igloo	Jj juice	Kk kite	Ll lion
Mm mouse	Nn nest	Oo octopus	Pp pizza
Qq quarter	Rr rainbow	Ss sun	Tt turtle
Uu umbrella	Vv violin	Ww watermelon	Xx xylophone
Yy yellow	Zz zebra	**ALPHABET CHART**	

Name: _____   Date: _____

THE ALPHABET

Listen and colour the letters

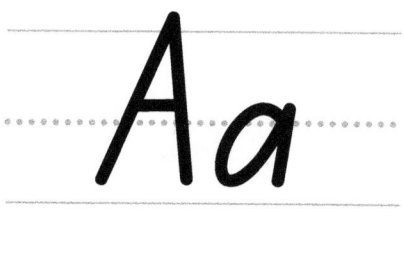

Ant

Practise your uppercase and lowercase As below:

Trace these words that begin with the letter A:

Bb

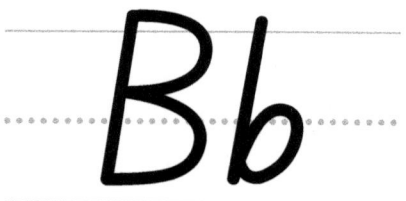

Bilby

Practise your uppercase and lowercase Bs below:

B B B B B B B B B

b b b b b b b b b b b

Bb Bb Bb Bb Bb Bb Bb

Trace these words that begin with the letter B:

Ball

Book

Banana

Bicycle

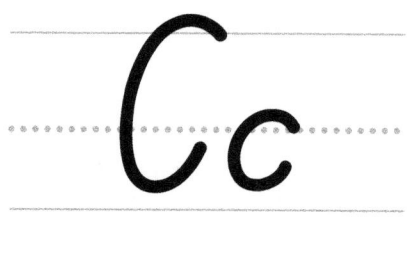

Cockatoo

Practise your uppercase and lowercase Cs below:

C C C C C C C C

c c c c c c c c c c

Cc Cc Cc Cc Cc Cc Cc

Trace these words that begin with the letter C:

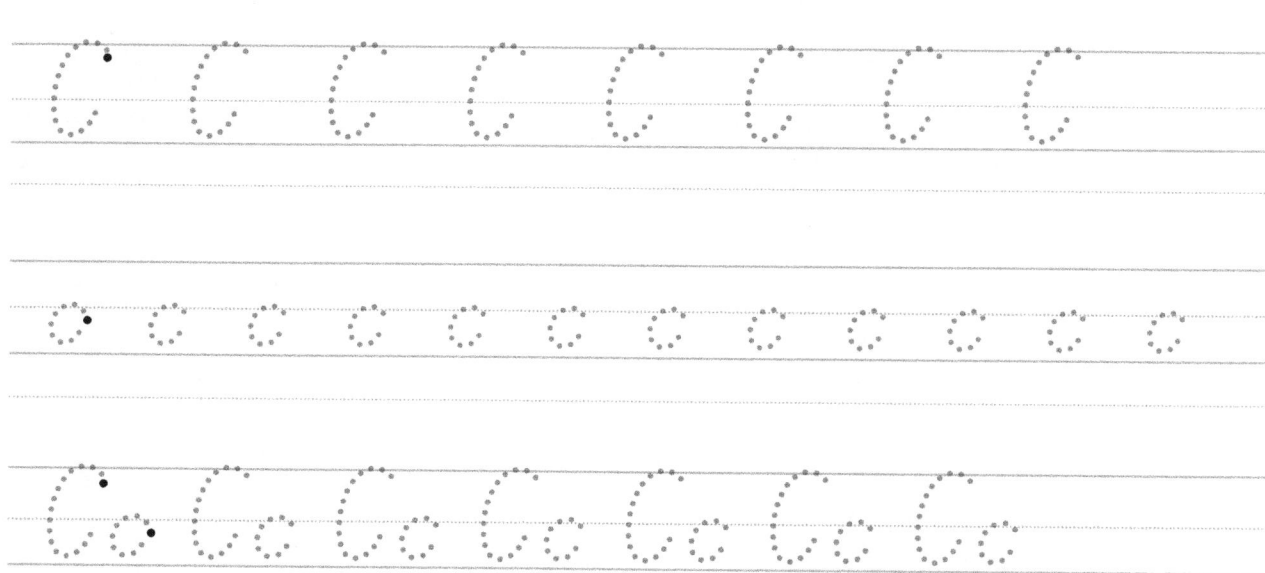

Cap

Cake

Circus

Crocodile

Dingo

Practise your uppercase and lowercase Ds below:

Trace these words that begin with the letter D:

Dice

Dress

Dolphin

Dinosaur

E e

Echidna

Practise your uppercase and lowercase Es below:

E E E E E E E E

e e e e e e e e e e e e

Ee Ee Ee Ee Ee Ee Ee

Trace these words that begin with the letter E:

Emu

Eggs

Earth

Envelope

Ff

Frog

Practise your uppercase and lowercase Fs below:

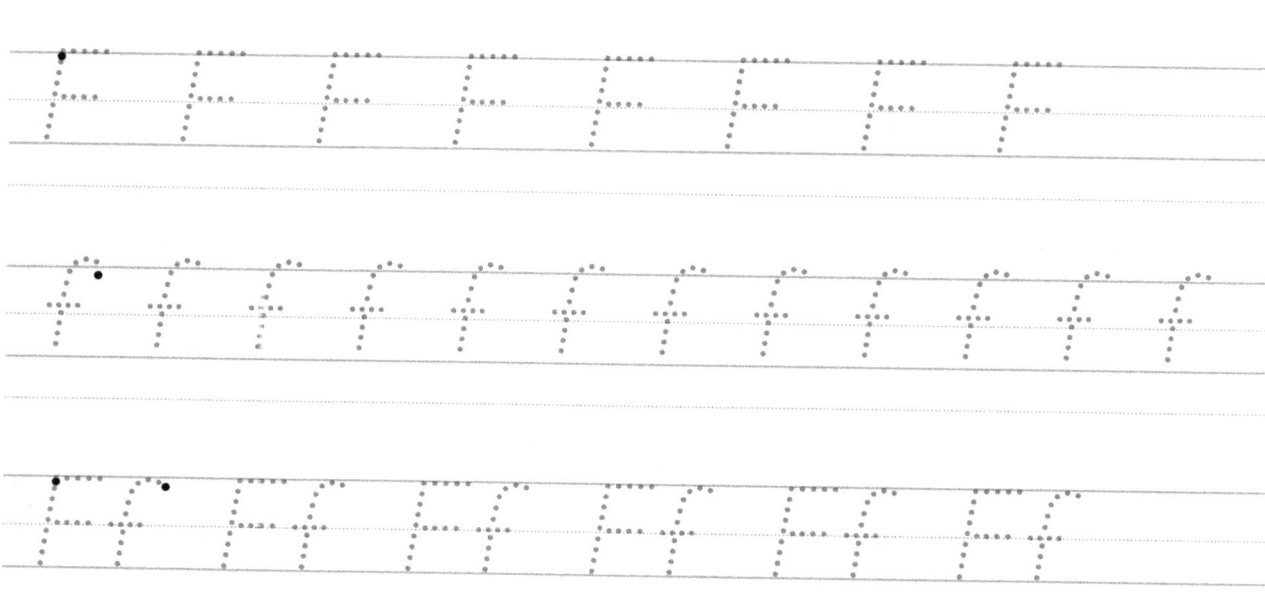

Trace these words that begin with the letter F:

Flag

Fish

Fence

Flower

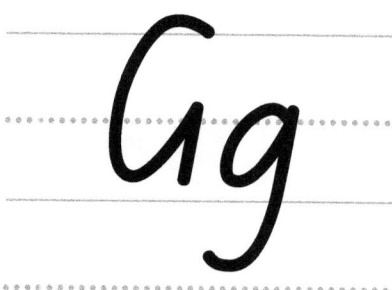 

Goanna

Practise your uppercase and lowercase Gs below:

Trace these words that begin with the letter G:

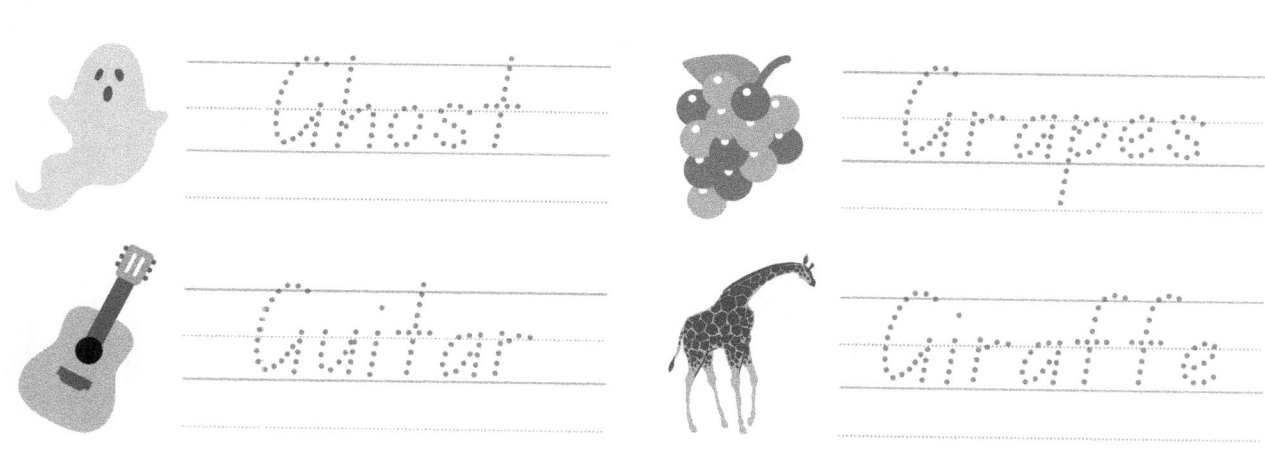

Hh

Huntsman Spider

Practise your uppercase and lowercase Hs below:

H H H H H H H H H H

h h h h h h h h h h h

Hh Hh Hh Hh Hh Hh Hh

Trace these words that begin with the letter H:

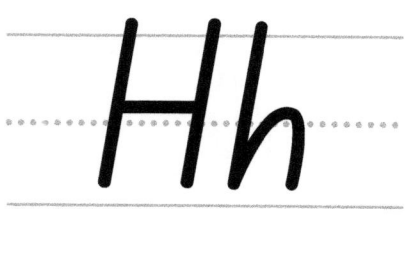

Hat

Hand

Horse

Hammer

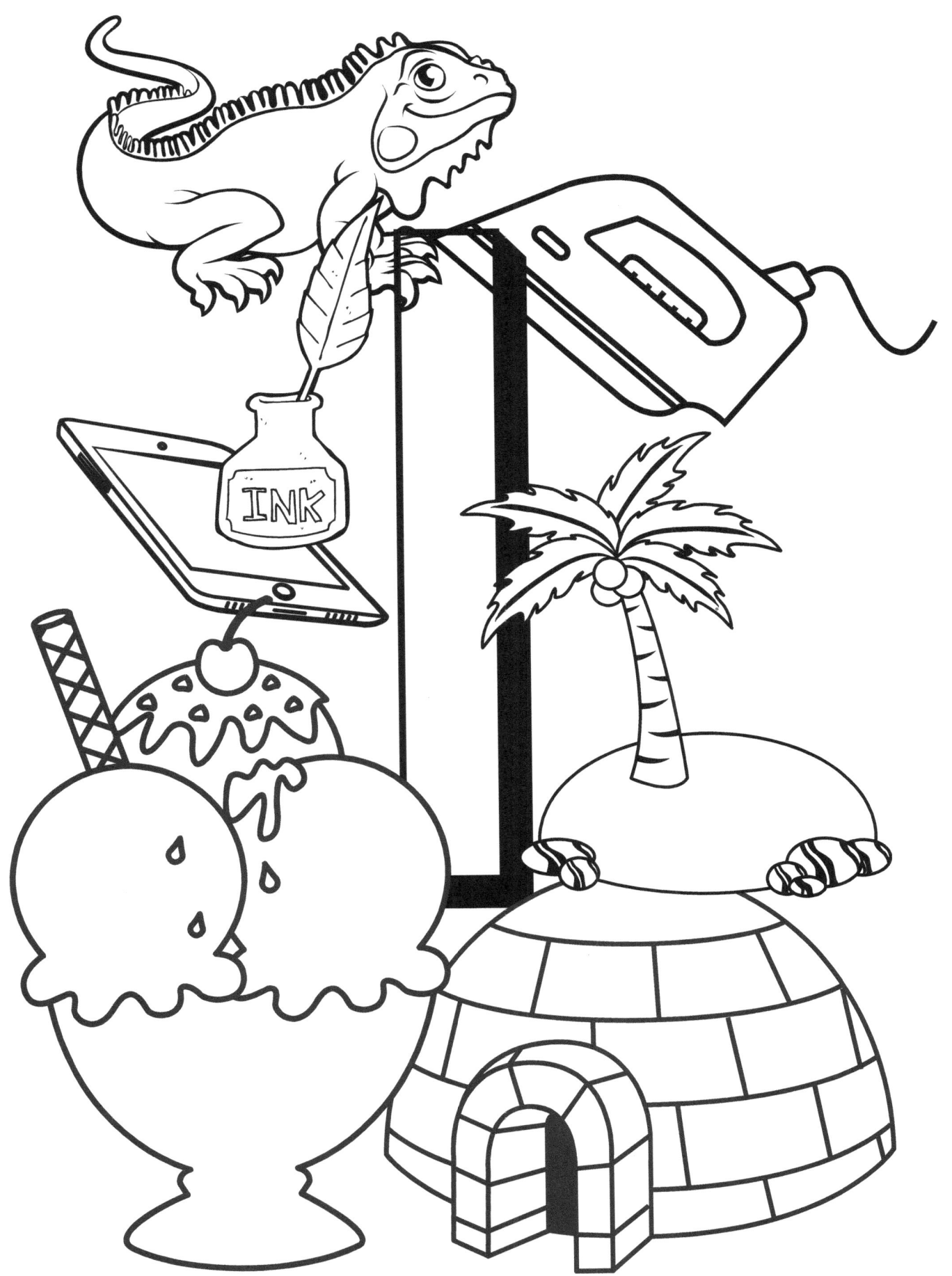

Ii

Ibis

Practise your uppercase and lowercase Is below:

I I I I I I I I I I

i i i i i i i i i i i

Ii Ii Ii Ii Ii Ii Ii Ii

Trace these words that begin with the letter I:

Ink

Iron

Island

Ice cream

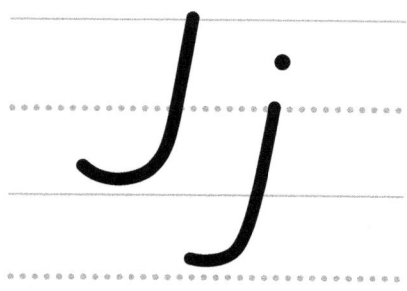

Jellyfish

Practise your uppercase and lowercase Js below:

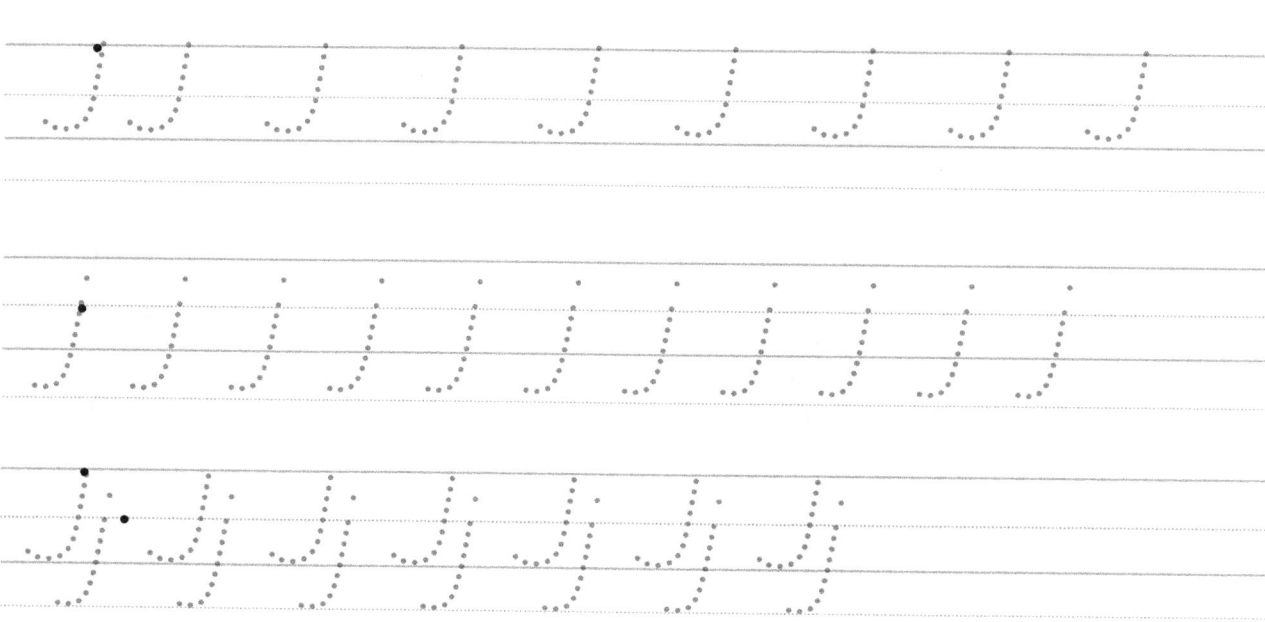

Trace these words that begin with the letter J:

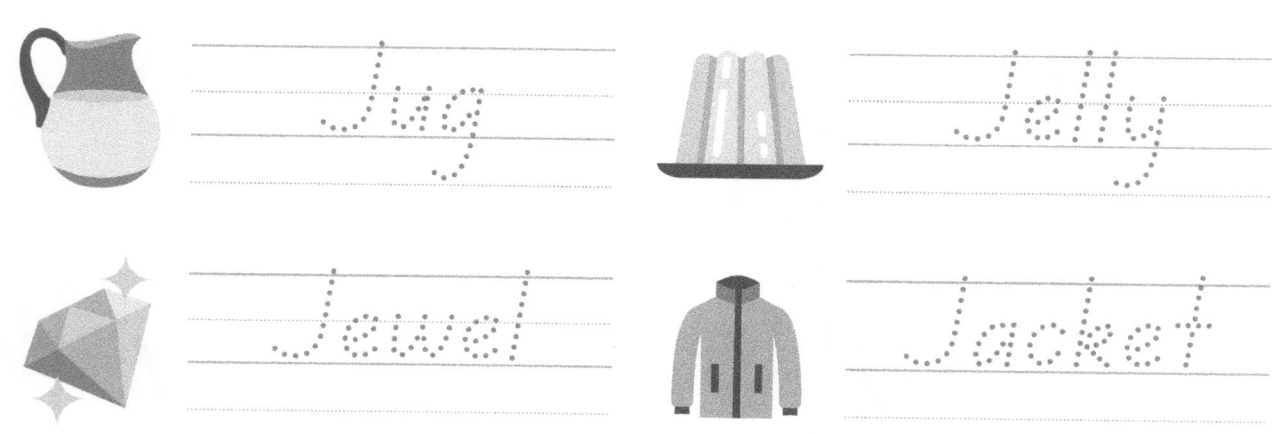

Jug

Jelly

Jewel

Jacket

Kk

Kangaroo

Practise your uppercase and lowercase Ks below:

Trace these words that begin with the letter K:

Key

Kite

Koala

Kettle

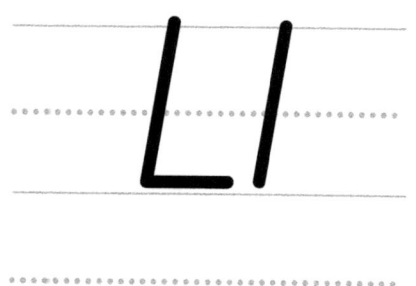

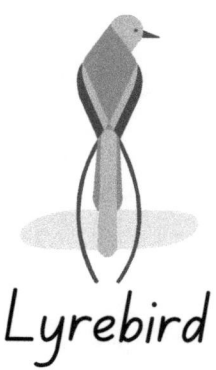

Lyrebird

Practise your uppercase and lowercase Ls below:

L L L L L L L L L

I I I I I I I I I

L L L L L L L L L

Trace these words that begin with the letter L:

Leg

Leaf

Lemon

Lightbulb

Magpie

Practise your uppercase and lowercase Ms below:

M M M M M M M M M M

m m m m m m m m m m

Mm Mm Mm Mm Mm Mm

Trace these words that begin with the letter M:

Map

Moon

Mango

Mountain

Nn

Numbat

Practise your uppercase and lowercase Ns below:

N N N N N N N N N N

n n n n n n n n n n

Nn Nn Nn Nn Nn Nn Nn

Trace these words thct begin with the letter N:

Nose

News

Noodles

Numbers

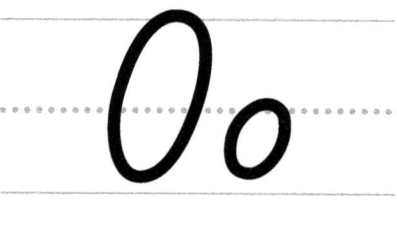

Oo

Orca

Practise your uppercase and lowercase Os below:

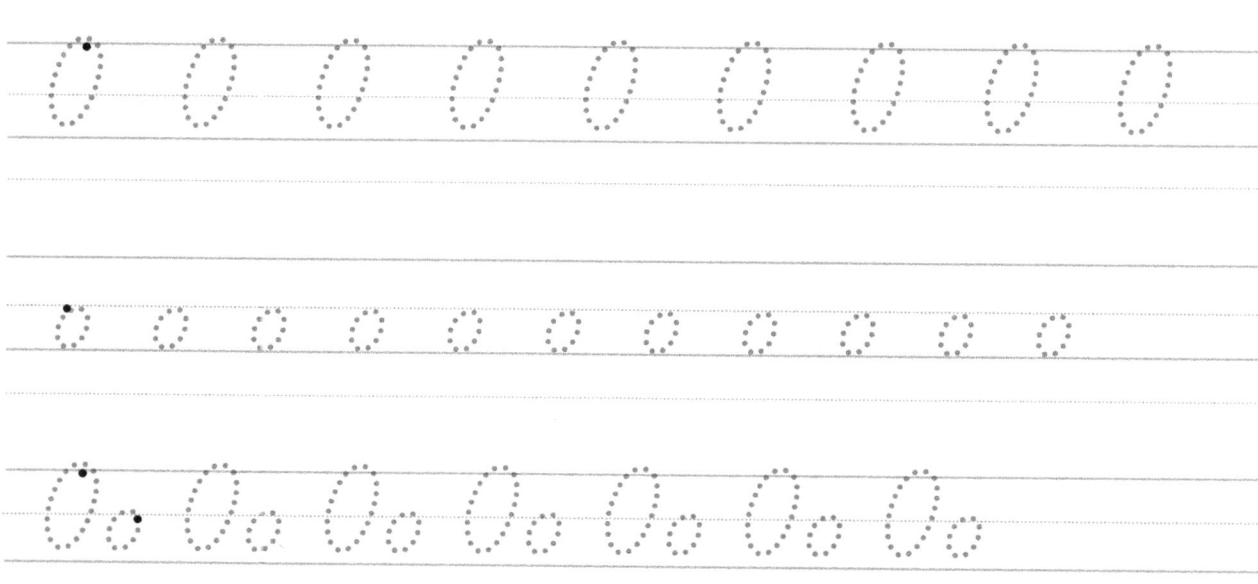

Trace these words that begin with the letter O:

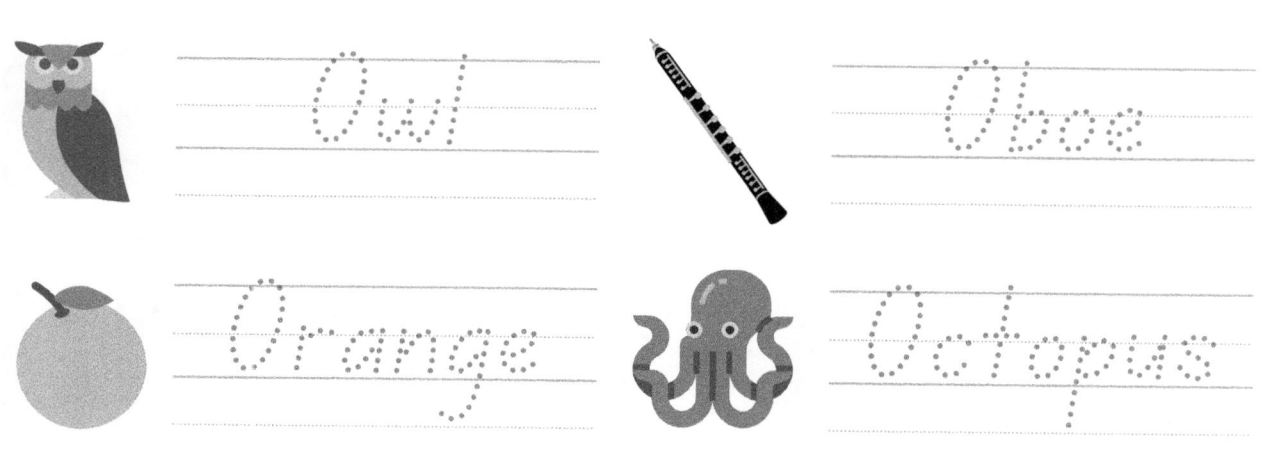

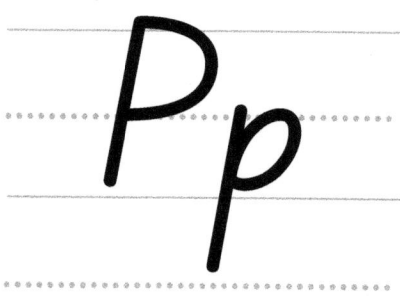

Platypus

Practise your uppercase and lowercase Ps below:

Trace these words that begin with the letter P:

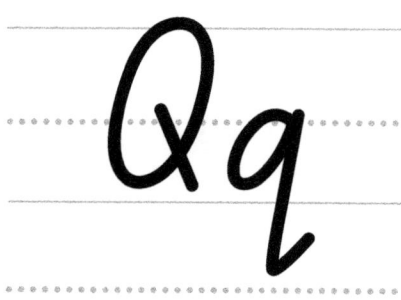

Qq

Quokka

Practise your uppercase and lowercase Qs below:

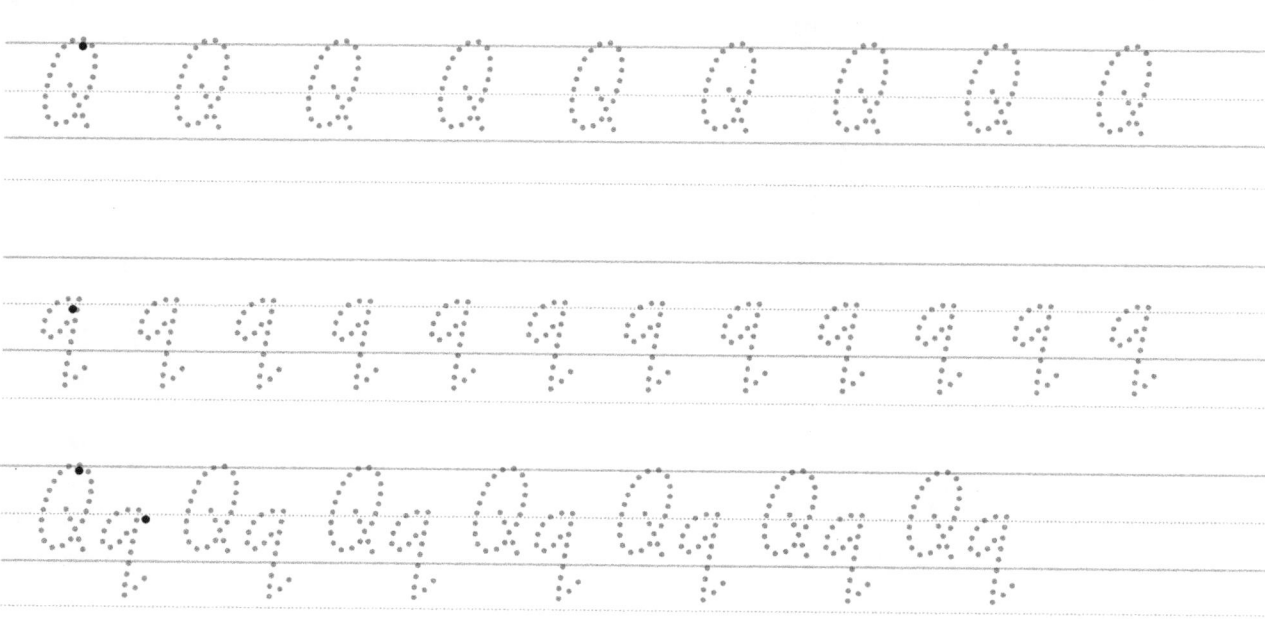

Trace these words that begin with the letter Q:

Quill

Quiche

Quarter

Question

Rr

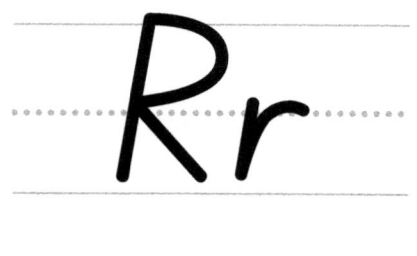

Rosella

Practise your uppercase and lowercase Rs below:

R R R R R R R R

r r r r r r r r r r

Rr Rr Rr Rr Rr Rr Rr Rr

Trace these words that begin with the letter R:

Run

Rain

Ruler

Rocket

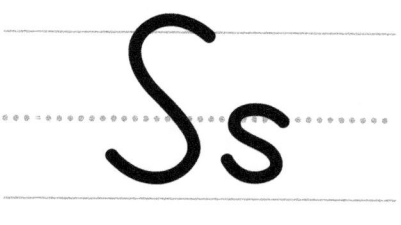

Sugar Glider

Practise your uppercase and lowercase Ss below:

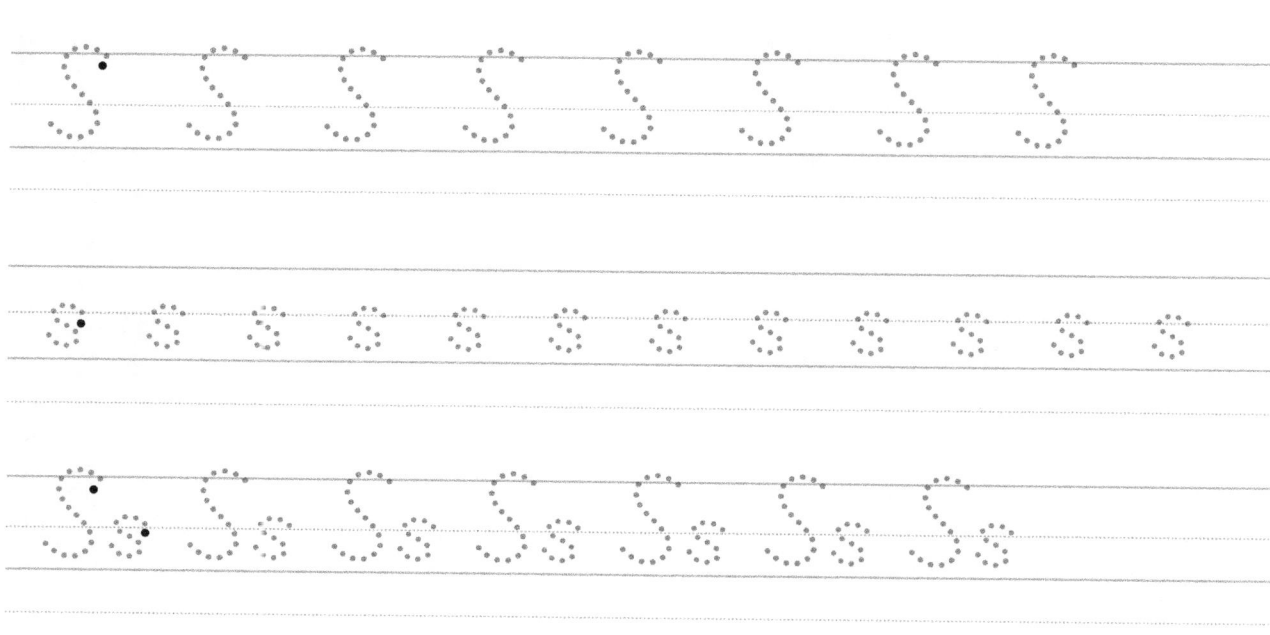

Trace these words that begin with the letter S:

Tt

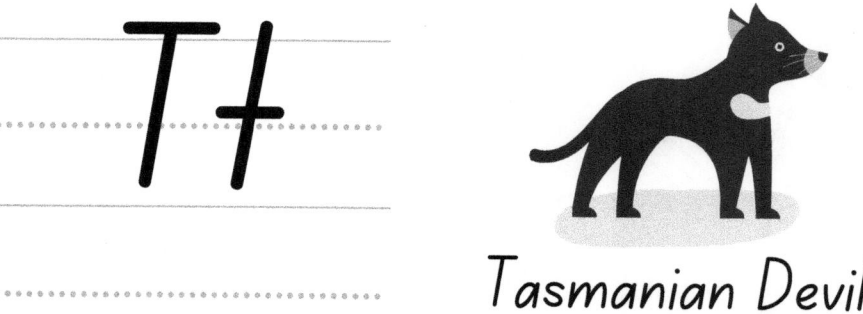

Tasmanian Devil

Practise your uppercase and lowercase Ts below:

Trace these words that begin with the letter T:

Tap

Taco

Tennis

Tractor

Urchin

Practise your uppercase and lowercase Us below:

Trace these words that begin with the letter U:

UFO

Uncle

Unicorn

Umbrella

V v

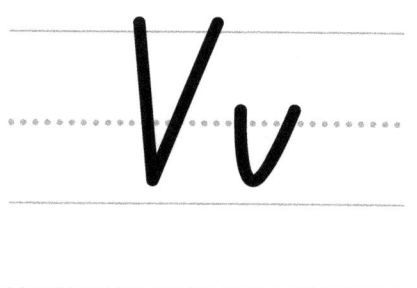

Velvet Gecko

Practise your uppercase and lowercase Vs below:

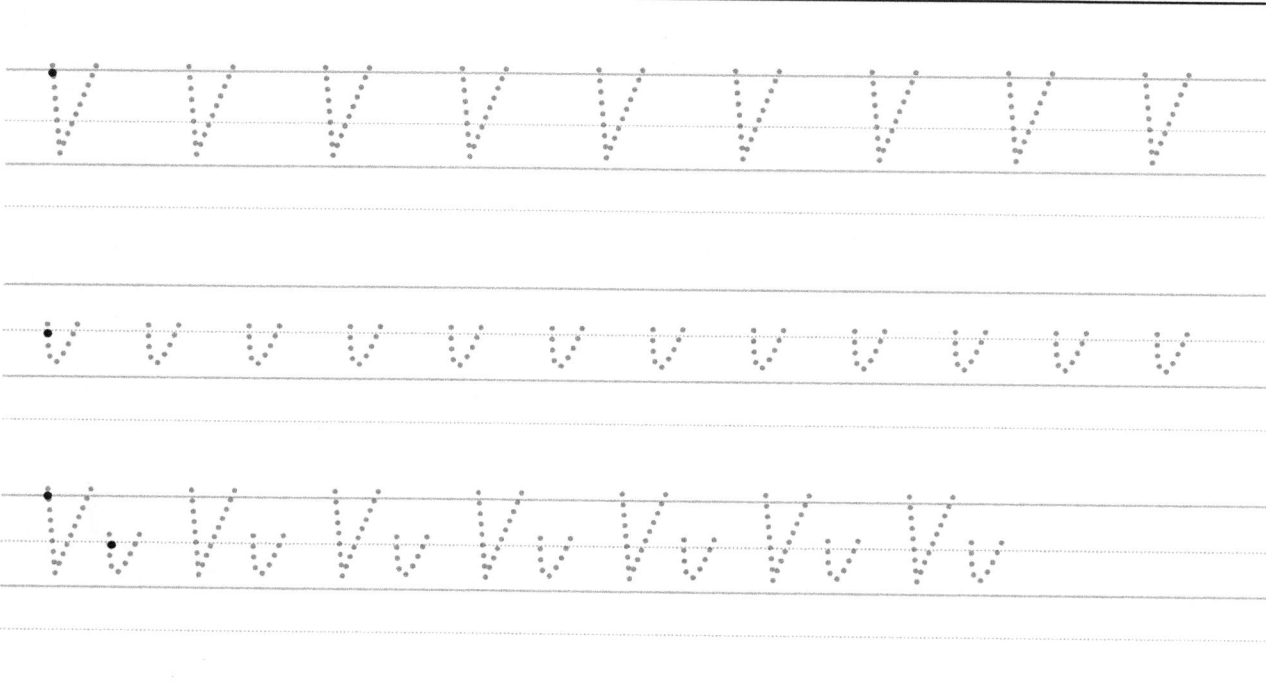

Trace these words that begin with the letter V:

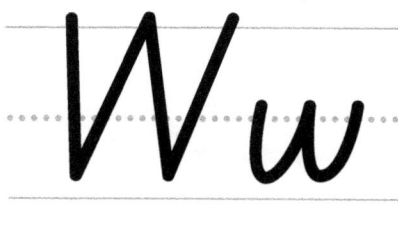

Wombat

Practise your uppercase and lowercase Ws below:

Trace these words that begin with the letter W:

Web

Wash

Whale

Window

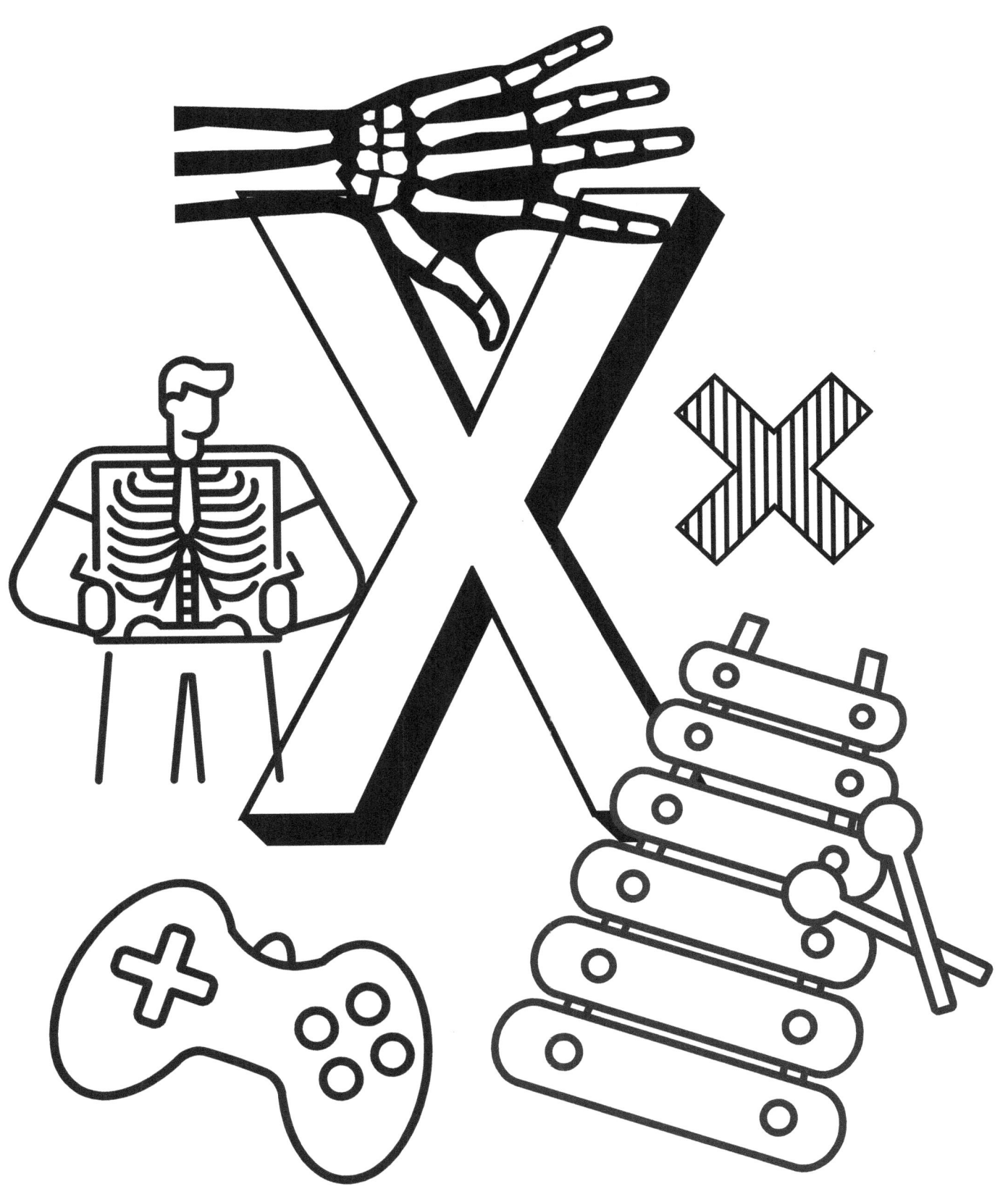

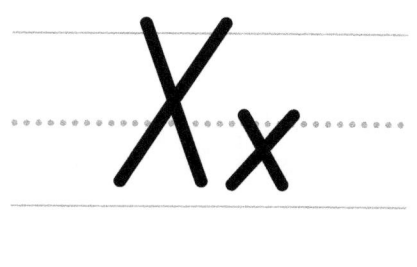

Xenicus

(New Zealand Wren)

Practise your uppercase and lowercase Xs below:

X X X X X X X X X X

X X X X X X X X X X

Xx Xx Xx Xx Xx Xx

Trace these words that begin with the letter X:

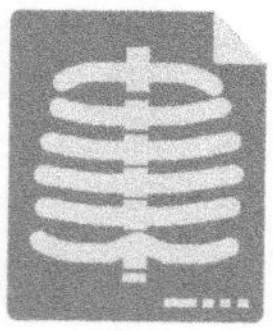

X-ray

Xiphias

Ximenia

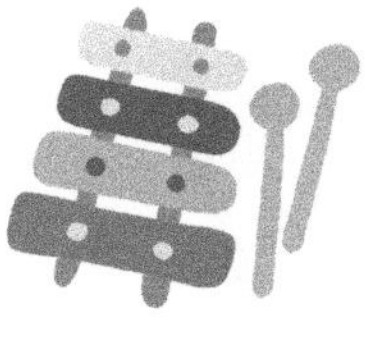

Xylophone

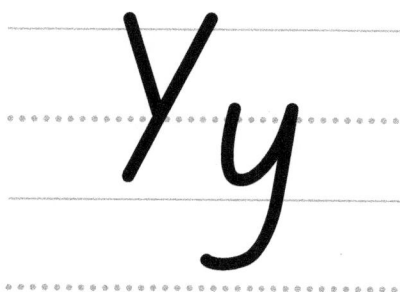

Yabby

Practise your uppercase and lowercase Ys below:

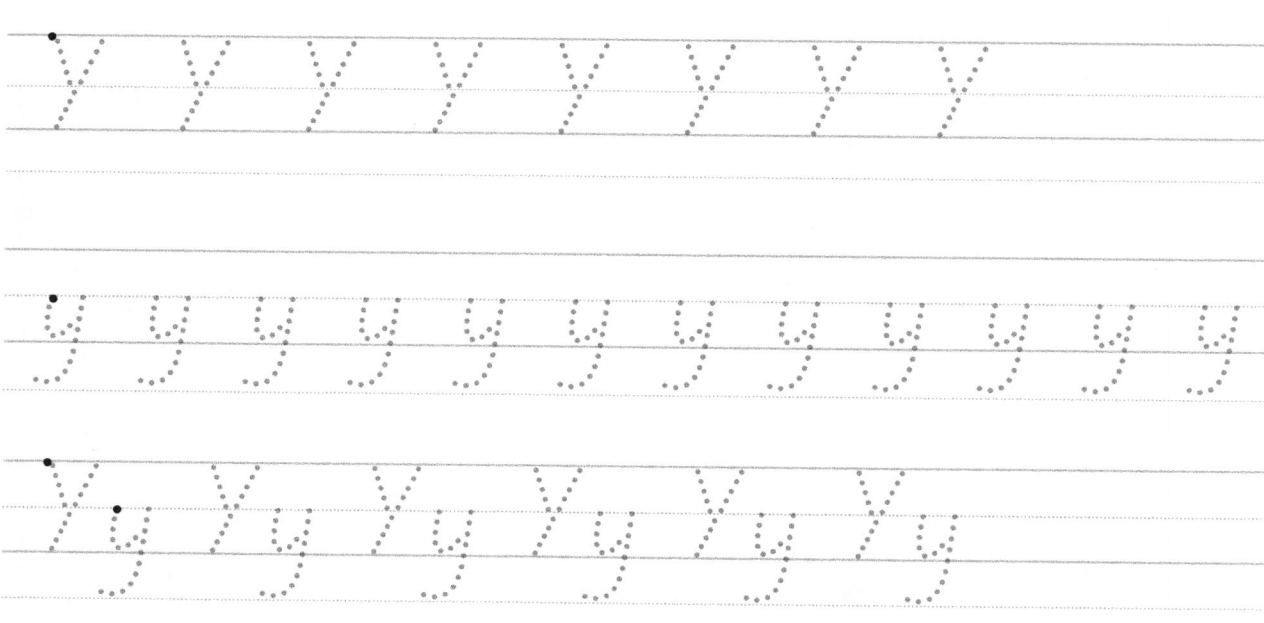

Trace these words that begin with the letter Y:

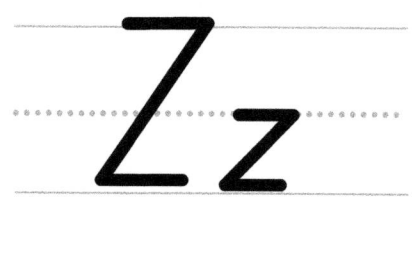

Zebra Finch

Practise your uppercase and lowercase Zs below:

Z Z Z Z Z Z Z Z Z Z

z z z z z z z z z z

Zz Zz Zz Zz Zz Zz Zz Zz

Trace these words that begin with the letter Z:

Zoo

Zebra

Zipper

Zucchini

Let's color-in our A-Z!

Alphabet
Tracing Practice

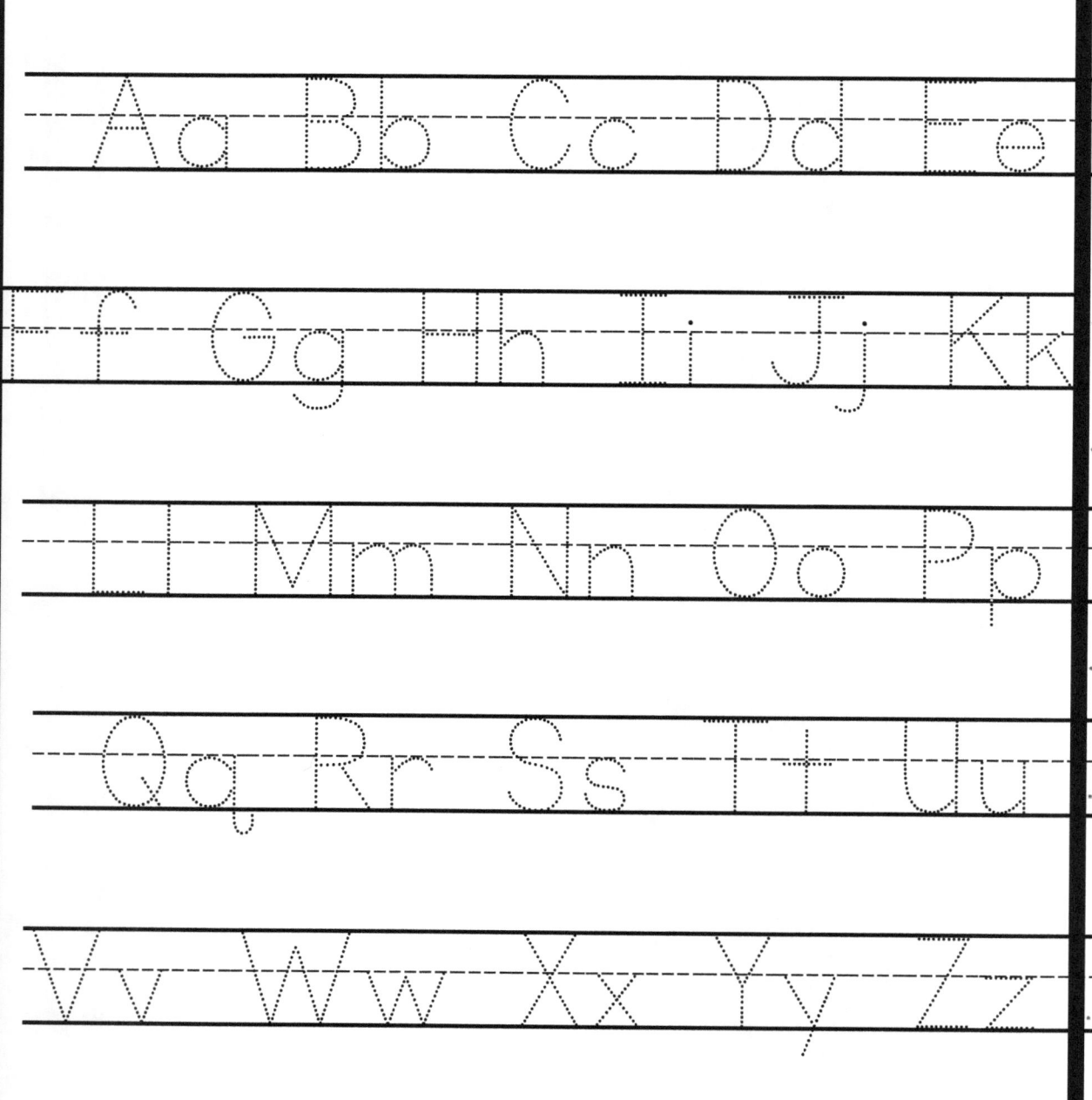

Aa Bb Cc Dd Ee

Ff Gg Hh Ii Jj Kk

Ll Mm Nn Oo Pp

Qq Rr Ss Tt Uu

Vv Ww Xx Yy Zz

Alphabet
Tracing Practice

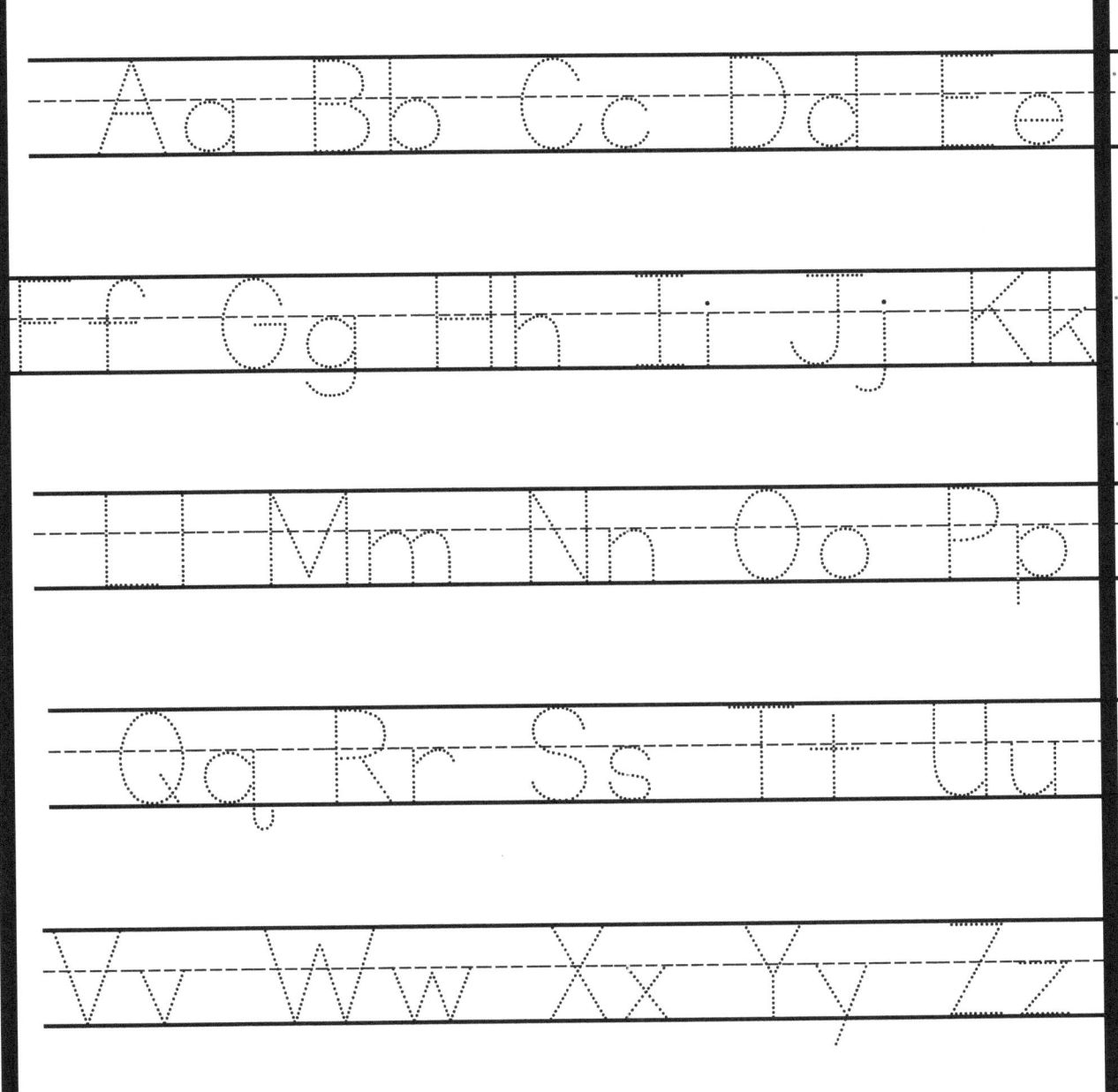

Aa Bb Cc Dd Ee

Ff Gg Hh Ii Jj Kk

Ll Mm Nn Oo Pp

Qq Rr Ss Tt Uu

Vv Ww Xx Yy Zz

I CAN WRITE MY ALPHABET

I CAN WRITE MY ALPHABET

I CAN WRITE MY ALPHABET

I CAN WRITE MY ALPHABET

www.ingramcontent.com/pod-product-compliance
Lightning Source LLC
Chambersburg PA
CBHW041520120626
46551CB00018B/2507